ZERO
WASTE

Kitchen

CRAFTY IDEAS FOR SUSTAINABLE KITCHEN SOLUTIONS

CHRISTINE LEECH
& EMMA FRIEDLANDER-COLLINS

DAVID & CHARLES

www.davidandcharles.com

Contents

Making a Sustainable Kitchen

The kitchen is the heart of our homes and finding ways to make it feel healthy and wholesome can be really important.

From leftover food scraps to the endless packaging that our food comes in, there's so much that goes on in a kitchen - it's probably the place in our homes where we generate the most waste. We can't tackle everything in one little book, so we won't be focussing on food waste or edible things, but we can help you to think of crafty solutions to help your kitchen become closer to zero waste.

In the main, these projects use classic craft skills like sewing and crochet, with a pinch of cutting, sticking and drilling thrown in for good measure. Learning how to do little bits of everything can become your toolkit to thinking creatively about how you can reuse everyday things, helping you towards a zero waste lifestyle.

Enjoy the journey!

Christine   Emma
x

Preparing your Zero Waste Kitchen

The kitchen is the busiest, most hard-working room in the house. It encompasses cooking, cleaning, shopping, eating, washing, living and growing. This little book couldn't possibly cover all of those things, so when we sat down to talk about what we wanted to share, we knew it would be how we use craft as part of our toolkit to reduce waste and live more sustainably.

Becoming confident with a glue gun, getting to grips with a sewing machine, knowing how to work a blanket stitch or even learning the basics of crochet are all really important skills that will help you to reimagine what waste materials can be. They allow you to transform a milk bottle into a cutlery caddy (packed lunches are an amazing quick win when it comes to reducing waste!), or make your own beeswax wraps. The more you craft, the more confident you become and the more opportunities you see in the things around you.

The other reason we wanted to focus on crafting instead of cooking or cleaning is that it's important to remember that crafting takes time. It's convenience that got us into this mess and crafting is a great way to reset that mindset. Crafting helps us to slow down, connects the head with the hands, and brings all sorts of benefits, not just to our wellbeing but to the planet. Adding a bit of hand sewing to your day instead of shopping online does wonders for the soul and develops a skill that can be used time and again.

This book then is about ways to remake things to help you in the kitchen. These are craft projects that can reduce the packaging coming out of your kitchen, and reuse things from around the house to reduce packaging going into your kitchen. They are here to inspire you to rethink the possibilities of waste, and of materials, and help you to build all the skills you need to live a zero waste lifestyle.

Making this book has been a pleasure and a delight. Emma says, 'When Christine suggested I have a go at making reusable popcorn bags I was so over-excited by having made popcorn in a fabric bag that I had to send her pictures!' We hope you enjoy it as much as we did and take as much delight in the surprises to be found in remaking things.

Tools and Materials

The basis of zero waste crafting is to reuse things that you have around you, so most of these projects can be made from things that you can find in your home. Once you've sourced your materials it's just a case of having a few basic tools and you're good to go.

MATERIALS

Fabric

Lots of the fabrics for these projects come from clothes. With 80% of clothes in second-hand shops ending up in landfill, it's much better to cut them up and turn them into a tea cosy than leave them hanging in a shop. But all of the projects in this book are about rethinking what existing objects are and what new life they can have with some simple transformations, so don't be afraid to get the scissors out.

Plastics

Make sure you clean out things like milk bottles thoroughly and then leave them somewhere to dry properly. The last thing you want is old milk going everywhere when you start cutting them up.

SEWING KIT

Fabric scissors

It's worth investing when it comes to fabric scissors, a good pair will give a nice clean cut and make your sewing life so much easier.

Sewing machine

A lot of these projects have an element of sewing and getting to grips with a sewing machine is invaluable if you're aiming for a zero waste lifestyle.

Hand sewing

Embroidery needles are ideal for so many things. They usually have a big enough eye to take things like yarn instead of thread, but they are sharp enough to get through tougher fabrics like denim.

OTHER TOOLS

Bradawl

This is an incredibly useful little tool designed specifically for making holes in things. Bradawls can be bought from DIY or craft stores and are inexpensive.

Crochet hooks

If you've never crocheted before a good average size hook for most yarns is a 5mm, grab one of these and you can use it on a DK yarn or an Aran weight. Hooks can be found in charity shops so there's no need to buy new.

Pinking shears

These are scissors that add a decorative edge to fabric and can also help prevent fraying.

ZERO WASTE MAKES

From cleaning cloths to ingenious storage, find a project that appeals to you from the following collection and start your journey to zero waste.

Upcycled Apron

This apron is made from a thrifted curtain and recycled gift wrap ribbon, but you can use anything. The idea is just to think about what you already have and how to reuse it.

"A sturdy cotton fabric is great for this apron, you could easily make it by cutting up old jeans and patching them together."

You will need

- 60 x 80cm (23½ x 31½in) piece of fabric for the apron
- 150cm (60in) ribbon
- 50 x 30cm (20 x 12in) piece of fabric for the pocket
- Fabric scissors
- Sewing machine or needle and thread

Create the apron shape. Fold the larger piece of fabric in half lengthways. On the top edge make a mark 25cm (10in) from the fold, and another 30cm (12in) down on the outside edge. Draw a curved line between the marks **(1)**.

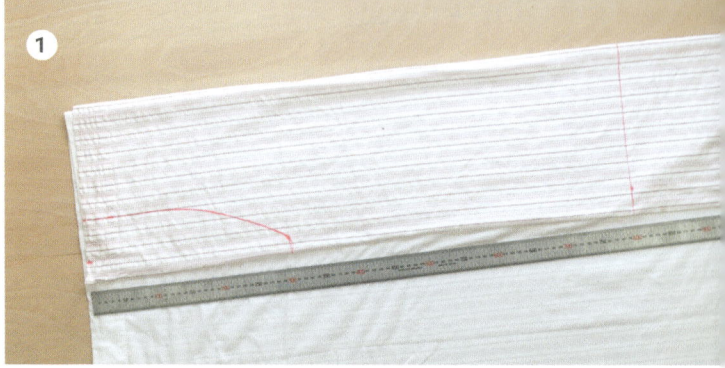

Cut out. Cut along the curved line through both thicknesses of fabric **(2)**.

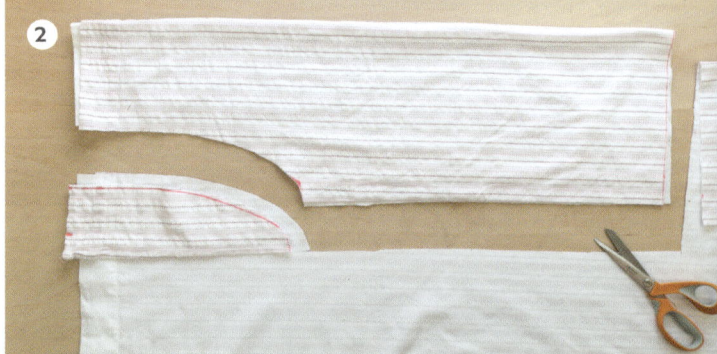

Hem the apron. Open out and hem all the raw edges with a 1cm (½in) seam (*see Techniques: Sewing*) **(3)**.

Make the strap and ties. Cut a 50cm (20in) length of ribbon and sew each end to the top corners of the apron **(4)**. Cut the remaining ribbon in half and sew a piece to either side, level with where the wearer's waist will be.

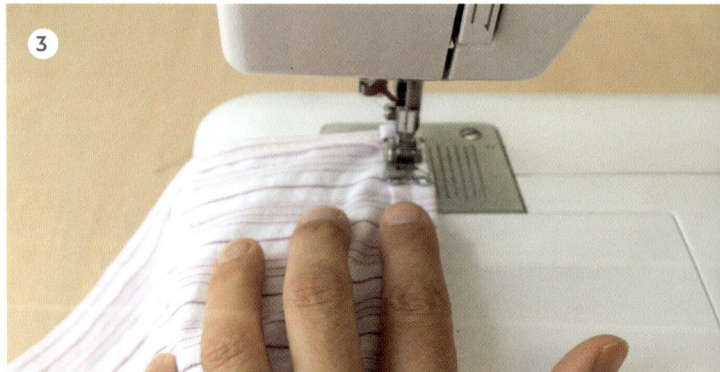

"If the idea of hemming something this size is intimidating you can always use pinking shears to cut out the fabric and leave it like that."

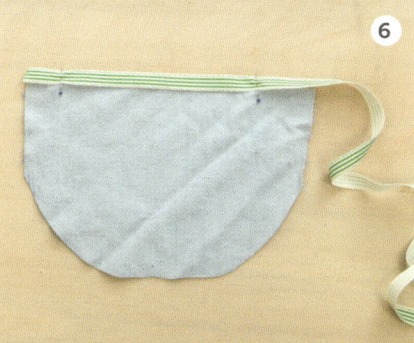

Cut out the pocket. Take the 50 x 30cm (20 x 12in) piece of fabric to make the pocket. You can keep the pocket as a rectangle or fold it in half and cut the corner into a curved shape **(5)**. Hem the top edge or follow the step below.

Trim with ribbon. If you have some spare ribbon, rather than hemming, you can use it to decorate the top edge of the pocket **(6)**. Just line up the raw edge of the fabric halfway up the ribbon, pin then sew it on one side, fold it over the raw fabric edge and sew it again on the other side.

Attach the pocket. On the wrong side of the pocket fabric, fold over and press the raw edges to create a 1.5cm (⅝in) hem and pin in place. Pin then sew the pocket to the apron **(7)**.

Beeswax Wraps

A brilliant alternative to cling film, these wraps can be made using any old cotton fabric you have lying around.

"You can make these any size you like by using tin foil layered up to the required size instead of using a baking tray, and because beeswax pellets are so cost effective you can make as many as you like."

You will need

- Greaseproof (parchment) paper
- Cotton fabric
- Baking tray or tin foil
- Fabric scissors or pinking shears
- Handful of beeswax pellets
- Iron

Cut the material out. Cut the fabric to the desired size, this wrap is 25 x 25cm (10 x 10in). You can use regular scissors as the beeswax will prevent fraying, or pinking shears to create a decorative edge **(1)**.

Prepare the fabric. Cut a piece of greaseproof (parchment) paper at least twice the width of your fabric and place it in the baking tray. Put the fabric on top, sprinkle with a good handful of beeswax – enough to sparingly cover the surface – and fold the rest of the paper on top **(2)**.

Iron in the wax. With the iron on its highest setting, rest it on top the paper. After a minute the pellets will begin to melt. Move the iron gradually over the surface and melt the wax into every bit of the material **(3)**.

Complete the wrap. Before it cools, peel off the paper and hang to dry **(4)**.

"Use the heat of your hands to set in place around whatever you want to wrap. These are not waterproof and shouldn't be used to wrap raw meat or things that can spread bacteria. Wipe clean with cool water (hot water will melt the wax). When they start to get a bit worn you can iron them again and they'll be as good as new."

Beeswax Lunch Bags

Waxed bags like these are perfect for packed lunches, and the less convenience food you buy when you're out, the less packaging you have to worry about.

"Like waxed wraps, these bags aren't waterproof and shouldn't be used to wrap raw meat or things that can spread bacteria. You can clean them with cool water, and they can be rejuvenated by re-ironing them."

You will need

- Greaseproof (parchment) paper
- Cotton fabric
- Baking tray or tin foil
- Fabric scissors
- Handful of beeswax pellets
- Iron
- Sewing machine or needle and thread

Cut and sew the material. Cut a piece of fabric 50 x 25cm (20 x 10in) **(1)**, fold in half with right sides together, and sew up the left and right sides.

Shape the bag. To create a nice wide bottom for the bag, pinch and flatten the corners out to make a triangle shape and sew across each one **(2)**.

Prepare the bag for wax. Cut a piece of greaseproof paper the same size as the bag and tuck it inside. Line the baking tray with greaseproof paper, sprinkle with pellets and lie the bag on top. Sprinkle another handful of pellets on top of the bag, cover with more paper **(3)**.

Iron in the wax. Put the iron on its highest setting and rest it on top the paper, after a minute the pellets will begin to melt. Move the iron carefully over the surface to melt the wax into every bit of the fabric. Before it cools, peel off the paper, remove the lining paper and hang to dry **(4)**.

Bias bound Washcloths

Making bias binding might seem like super advanced 'seamstressing' but it's really simple to master and can open up a world of upcycling, reusing and remaking.

"Bias bound edges are a great way to avoid bulky hems, create colourful and contrasting edges and use up all those little fabric scraps that might otherwise be headed for the bin."

You will need

- Scraps of fabric of a similar weight, for the binding
- Fabric scissors
- Iron
- Old towel, for the cloth fabric
- Sewing machine or needle and thread

Find the bias. Fabric has a 'warp' (the lengthways yarn) and a 'weft' (the yarn woven side to side around the weft). If you pull the fabric in either of these directions there's not a lot of elasticity, but if you pull it diagonally – on the bias – then you'll see it becomes stretchy. This stretch is ideal for sewing around curves and edges and is what makes bias binding so useful **(1)**.

Cut out the pieces. Once you've found the bias, mark out pieces 5cm (2in) wide and cut them out, ensuring the stretch goes up the middle of the fabric piece **(2)**. Cut out as many pieces as you can from a variety of fabrics.

Sew strips together. Place two fabric pieces together with the right sides facing and sew along the short edge. Repeat to make a long strip **(3)**.

Press into shape. Press the seams flat and then with the fabric lengthways and wrong side facing up, fold over the raw edges so that they meet in the middle and press in place **(4)**.

Cut the towel and pin the fabric. Cut the towel into 25cm (10in) squares. Open up one edge of the bias binding and pin in place so the raw edges line up **(5)**.

To go round the corners. When pinning the binding to the cloth, when you get to about 2cm (¾in) from the corner, fold the binding towards you, pinch the corner in place and then fold the binding back and pin in place along the next edge.

Sew in place. Sew along the fold line of the bias binding **(6)**.

Trim and sew again. The towel will be bulky so trim the towel edge back as close to the sewn line as you can, then fold the bias binding around the raw edge, pin in place and sew as close as you can to the folded edge of the binding **(7)**.

Fruit Bag Scourer

While the supermarkets get their acts together to reduce plastic packaging, you can take advantage of some of it. Save the net bags from your fruit and veg to transform into something useful.

Prepare the bags. When opening your fruit bags, carefully snip off the silver tags at either end and give them a rinse off. You will need a small tube bag – a garlic bulb bag is ideal – for the main container bag **(1)**.

Close one end. Insert a crochet hook into the netting at the right corner of one of the open ends, draw up a loop and work a chain stitch (*see Techniques: Crochet*). Work a row of double crochet along the open edge and slip stitch to finish **(2)**.

Stuffing the scourer. Fold and then roll the other bags and stuff the main container bag **(3)**.

Close the other end. Snip off any excess netting and stuff that into the container bag too, and then repeat the crochet steps to close the end **(4)**.

"We have used crochet to seal the ends but you could hand sew the ends or use a bit of bias binding (see Bias Bound Washcloths) for extra colour."

Jumper Tea Cosy

This cheerful cosy is perfect for a teapot for two and provides a new life for an old, pre-loved jumper.

Cut out the cosy. Turn the jumper inside out and fold in half lengthways. Measure the height of your teapot and add about 10cm (4in). From the bottom of the jumper draw a semicircle the height of your measurement, then cut out the shape with sharp fabric scissors **(1)**.

Sew together. Sew around the curved edge with a sewing machine or by hand **(2)**.

Blanket stitch. Turn the cosy the right way out and work a blanket stitch (*see Techniques: Embroidery*) around the curved edge **(3)**. Then blanket stitch the two layers on each side of the bottom edge together too.

Split stitch. Use the ruler to mark straight lines with the washable pen across the cosy and then use a split stitch (*see Techniques: Embroidery*) to embroider the coloured lines. **(4)**

You will need

- Old jumper
- Washable pen
- Ruler
- Fabric scissors
- Sewing machine or needle and thread
- Embroidery threads or yarn and suitable sized needle

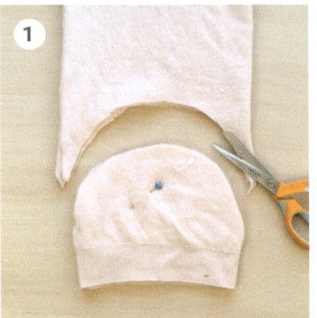

"This is a great project to experiment with embroidery stitches. We've suggested split stitch, but feel free to play and explore different things."

Universal Crochet Pot Cover

Re-using containers to create handy pots is great but can look a bit messy. Crochet co-ordinating covers for any size of pot to bring a bit of classy unity to your kitchen.

"Crochet is a brilliant tool in your upcycling arsenal, and this pattern is perfect for beginners as it uses just one stitch."

You will need

- Craft knife
- Plastic bottle
- Cotton yarn
- A suitable sized crochet hook
- Washable pen
- Contrasting yarn and yarn needle

Cut the bottle. You can use jars for this, but if you want to use up those plastic bottles too, take a craft knife and neatly cut to the desired height **(1)**.

Crochet the bottom (see Techniques: Crochet).

Ch 4 and ss into first st to make a loop.

Rnd 1: Dc 6 in the loop.

Rnd 2: *2dc, dc* rpt to end. (12)

Rnd 3: *2dc, dc 2* rpt to end. (18)

Rnd 4: *2dc, dc 3* rpt to end. (24)

Rnd 5: *2dc, dc 4* rpt to end. (30)

Continue adding an extra stitch each round until your circle neatly covers the bottom of your pot **(2)**.

Crochet the edges. Dc in each stitch and keep going until it is the same height as the jar. Once it is tall enough, *dc2tog, dc to whatever number of stitches you got to* and fasten off **(3)**.

Add some features. Leave your pots plain or use a little contrasting thread to add some features. This smiling face design is drawn on with washable pen and embroidered using back stitch (see Techniques: Embroidery) **(4)**.

Cat Head Trivet

We love a trivet – although many work surfaces are supposed to cope with hot saucepan bottoms, we're always a bit wary! Smaller versions of the cat's head can work as coasters, or you could go large and make a set of place mats.

"As an alternative to the cat shape, experiment with winding and stitching the plait in different ways to create different animals. Fish, bunny heads and even words are all possible with a bit of thought."

You will need

- Three colours of t-shirt yarn, about 2m (2¼yd) of each. (*See Techniques: T-shirt Yarn*)
- Needle and thread

Make a long plait from the t-shirt yarns. Tie them at one end to start, then when finished instead of knotting the other end, stitch the three yarns together with a couple of over stitches – just wrap the thread around the plait and sew through it a couple of times to secure. Bend the last 3cm (1¼in) of the plait back on itself – fold it so it sits alongside rather than on top of the previous piece of plait. Stitch the two pieces of plait together using over stitches between the two pieces **(1)**.

Keep bending and coiling the plait around itself. Sew the plaits together as you coil. Working on the underside of the trivet, stitch through the outer strand of one plait and then through the neighbouring strand of the adjacent plait. Bring the needle and thread out and over to the initial strand then repeat. **(2)**.

Add the ears. When you are 40cm (15¾in) from the end, form a pointed shape with about 10cm (4in) of the plait. Stitch in place **(3)** then 4cm (1½in) later make a second ear. If you want to make the ears extra pointed, sew a couple of stitches to pull the plait together at the point of the ear to keep its shape.

Continue winding and stitching the rest of the plait around the head. When you reach the end undo the knot, fold the strands over themselves to hide the raw ends, then sew to the trivet to secure **(4)**. Work on a flat surface to avoid the trivet curling up into a bowl (although this method does make great bowls too - if you want to do that, just gradually curl and stitch the plait upwards instead of flat).

"Use the cat's ear to hang the trivet up when not in use."

Reusable Wipes

You really don't need new cloths or paper towels for wiping up spills. Just hang a stack of these wipes somewhere convenient in your kitchen, and chuck them in the machine with your regular wash after use.

"Our favourite garments to use for these wipes are super absorbent ones, such as t-shirts and soft flannel shirts."

You will need

- 24 x 36cm (9½ x 14¼in) of card for a template
- Fabric scissors
- Soft, absorbent fabrics: a mix of t-shirt material, brushed flannel, 100% cotton and linen garments
- A length of t-shirt yarn (*see Techniques: T-shirt Yarn*)
- Sewing machine or needle and thread

Cut the fabric. Using the card template, cut two pieces of fabric per wipe. Cut one from t-shirt fabric and one from cotton/linen or flannel. **(1)**.

Make the hanging loop. Cut a 10cm (4in) length of t-shirt yarn, fold in half and place the looped end on the body of the cloth with the two cut ends sticking out by about 3cm (1¼in) **(2)**.

Sandwich the fabrics. Place the second piece of fabric over the first and pin around each side **(3)**. Make sure you have a pin holding the hanging loop in place. Sew around the edge with a 1cm (½in) seam allowance. Leave a 10cm (4in) turning gap in one long side.

Turn right side out. The hanging loop will pop out. Press, taking care to fold the raw edges of the turning gap inwards **(4)**. Stitch a row of topstitch (*see Techniques: Sewing*) with a 5mm (¼in) seam allowance around all four sides, stitching the turning gap closed as you go.

"If your fabric scraps aren't large enough, sew pieces together (try to stick to similar weights and fabric types if you do this)."

Wrap for Life

These reusable sandwich wraps are made from the strong woven plastic that Bags for Life or Ikea blue bags are made from. They'll ensure your overflowing egg mayonnaise sandwich doesn't contaminate the rest of your lunch.

Make the template. Draw a 14cm (5½in) square onto the card. Enlarge the wrap template (*see Templates*) by 400% so the straight edge is 14cm (5½in). Copy then cut out this template and use it to draw four flaps around the square **(1)**. Cut the card template out.

Cut your chosen bag into flat sections. Using a pencil draw around the template onto the reverse of one piece of the bag **(2)**. Cut out the wrap shape using scissors or pinking shears for a decorative edge.

Cut the fastener. With the two sides of hook-and-loop fastener stuck together, cut a 2cm (¾in) piece (or if you are using the self-adhesive dots fix a pair together). Fold the two side flaps and then the lower flap inwards **(3)**. Stick the hook-and-loop fastener to the underside of the remaining flap about 3cm (1¼in) from the top. Fold the flap closed and press down firmly, this will transfer the second half of the hook-and-loop fastener to the lower flap. Remember you want to get a sandwich inside so don't seal the wrap too tightly!

You will need

- 40 x 40cm (15¾ x 15¾in) of card for template
- Fabric scissors or pinking shears
- Pencil
- Self-adhesive hook-and-loop strips or dots
- Bag for Life/Ikea blue bag

"Creating an initial template from card means you can make several of these wraps in a matter of minutes."

Denim Storage Baskets

Once you've made one, you'll find dozens of uses for these handy baskets – you'll be making them for every room in your house in no time!

"The uses for these baskets are endless – from somewhere to store potatoes or apples, to a place to fling your dirty tea towels."

You will need

- One pair of jeans per basket, medium weight, at least 38 x 86cm (15 x 34in)
- Men's shirt, for lining fabric in medium to thick cotton or flannel, at least 40 x 86cm (15¾ x 34in)
- Cardboard
- Large plastic padded envelope
- Sewing machine and thread
- Measuring tape
- Fabric scissors

Decide on the height of your basket. Measure that height from the jeans cuff upwards. The jeans cuff will become the top. Mark, then cut both legs off. Cut open each leg of the jeans along the inner seam, or whichever seam doesn't have the distinctive jeans topstitching **(1)**.

Make a long rectangle. Pin the two rectangles together, right sides facing, along one edge. Sew with a 1cm (½in) seam allowance. Open then press the seam. Next, sew the seam flat with a row of topstitching (*see Techniques: Sewing*) **(2)**.

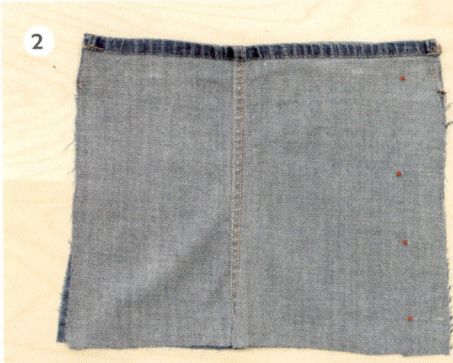

Create the handles. Cutting as close to the seam as possible remove the waistband from the jeans. Cut in half and remove buttons and belt loops. Pin each handle on the basket, equidistant from the original jean seam. Machine sew in place with a square of topstitch **(3)**.

Form the sides. Fold the long rectangle in half, right sides facing, pin and sew the remaining straight edge to form a tube with a 1cm (½in) seam allowance **(4)**. Finish with a row of topstitching.

"Your basket's dimensions will be determined by the size of the jeans you use. Look for large men's straight-leg jeans (it's harder to get square pieces of fabric from flares or boot cut legs)."

Determine the size of the base. Use a tape measure to check the circumference of your tube **(5)**. Use the formula: circumference divided by 3.14 to determine the diameter of your base circle. For example, if your tube has a circumference of 84cm (33in) then the diameter of the base will be 27cm (10½in), which is handily about the size of a dinner plate!

Cut the base. From the remaining jeans cut another piece of denim big enough for your base circle and draw round a dinner plate, or another suitable circular template. Cut out with a 5mm (¼in) seam allowance **(6)**.

Attach the base. Starting at one seam carefully pin the base to the tube right sides facing. It's best to use a lot of pins to get it neat **(7)**. If you reach the end and you have excess base you'll need to start again and trim the base slightly smaller – sometimes this can be a bit of trial and error. When pinned in place, hand sew a line of basting stitches 1cm (½in) in from the edge, then remove the pins. This makes it easier to fit under the sewing machine foot. Carefully machine sew with a 5mm (¼in) seam allowance, then remove the basting stitches. Turn the basket right side out and press the base seam.

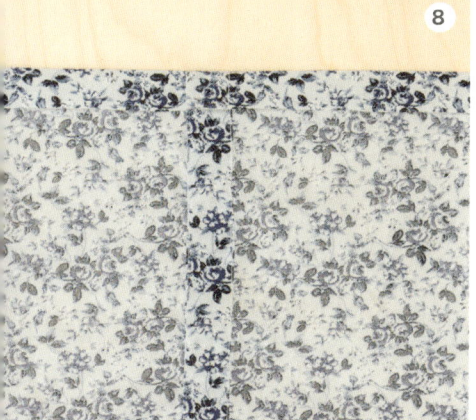

The lining is made in the same way as the outer basket. The button placket of the shirt is used to create the opening where you will insert the padded envelope. Keep this buttoned up as you make the lining. Cut and sew the shirt to make a rectangle the same dimensions as your outer basket but add 2cm (¾in) to the height. Fold and press a 2cm (¾in) hem along one long edge **(8)**. This will become the top edge of the lining. Fold the rectangle in half, pin and sew along the short edge to make a tube. Make and add the circular bottom as before.

Insert the lining. Keeping the lining wrong side out, insert it into the basket. Line up the turned top edge of the lining just below the hemmed top edge of the basket. Pin and then sew with a 5mm (¼in) seam allowance. For invisible stitching use a thread the colour of the denim as your topstitch and one the colour of your lining for the bobbin **(9)**.

Add stability to your basket. Pull the lining out of the basket and open the buttons. Cut a cardboard circle 1cm (½in) smaller than the base and insert it through the hole, manipulate it so that it sits between the outer basket and the lining. Open out the padded envelope and cut it 1cm (½in) smaller than the dimension of your basket. Insert it into the opening and manipulate it so it sits nicely in the outer basket. Close the buttons and push the lining back into the basket securing the padded envelope in position **(10)**.

"Many padded envelopes (commonly known as 'jiffy bags') aren't recyclable but their combination of strength and flexibility make them the ideal thing to give these baskets structure. Bubble wrap also works for the sides, but cardboard is far better for the base as it is more rigid."

Bird Pot Holder

This pot holder is great for hot saucepan handles and it can double up as a trivet to protect your work surfaces.

"When sewing through several layers, you need a fabric that's thick but not too tightly woven. Sweatshirting, flannel or linen works well."

You will need

- An old towel
- Thick fabric for the outer bird
- Thinner fabric (shirting) for the lining
- Small length of t-shirt yarn (*see Techniques: T-shirt Yarn*) or ribbon
- Fabric scissors
- Sewing machine or needle and thread

Prepare the fabric. Copy and print out the templates (*see Templates*) to the correct size. Cut a piece from each of the three fabrics for each of the template pieces. Leave plenty of excess fabric all around the template shapes.

For the head and tail. Layer up the fabric in this order: towel, outer fabric right side up, then lining fabric right side down. Place the head and tail templates on top and draw round **(1)**.

Sew the head. Pin the three layers of fabric together, then machine sew along the curve of the neck from A–B **(2)**, and then repeat with the curve of the tail.

Trim the excess fabric. Trim along the sewn edge down to a 5mm (¼in) allowance **(3)**. Turn the lining fabric over so it covers the towel, hiding the sewn edge, then press.

For the body. Layer the fabric in this order: towel, main fabric right side up, then add the tail and the head with their main fabric right side down. Position the tail first, then the head partly overlapping as shown **(4)**. Finally place the body lining fabric right side down on top, sandwiching the wings and head.

Cut out the layers of fabric for the body. Place the template on top of the lining fabric and draw round. Remove the template and pin through all layers **(5)**.

Add a hanging loop. Cut an 8cm (3¼in) length of t-shirt yarn, fold in half then place it loop side down in between the two layers of outer fabric at the top of the head **(6)**.

Sew around the bird. Starting at the base of the bird, machine sew about 5mm (¼in) in from the drawn line **(7)**. Stop just after you reach the end of the head, leaving a hole for turning out the right way.

Trim the fabric and finish. Reduce the excess fabric to a 5mm (¼in) seam allowance. Carefully turn right side out **(8)**, then fold the raw edges in and hand sew up the hole.

"It's a nice touch to finish the bird by adding an eye with an old spare shirt button."

Net Produce Bags

These produce bags are great for keeping your fruit and veg organised in your fridge. Don't forget to take them shopping with you to reduce the need for plastic bags.

"Make lots of bags in different sizes using combinations of net and fabric. Some could have fabric backs and net fronts, some could be all net!"

You will need

- Old net curtain
- Cotton fabric
- Fabric scissors
- Sewing machine or needle and thread
- About 60cm (23½in) of t-shirt yarn (*see Techniques: T-shirt Yarn*)
- Safety pin

1

2

Cut the fabric. Cut two 12 x 34cm (4¾ x 13½in) rectangles from cotton fabric and two 28 x 34cm (11 x 13½in) rectangles from the net curtain.

Stitch the fabrics together. Pin the fabric rectangles to the net rectangles along one short edge. Zig zag stitch along the raw edge and then sew with a 5mm (¼in) seam allowance **(1)**.

Place both pieces together right sides out. Pin around edges leaving top open. Sew with a 5mm (¼in) seam allowance starting and stopping where the fabric meets the net. Trim the seam allowance down to 3mm (⅛in) **(2)**.

Turn the bag inside out and press. Pin again and sew with a 5mm (¼in) seam allowance making sure you catch all the raw edges of the previous seam allowance inside the new seam. Turn right side out and press **(3)**.

Hem the fabric drawstring channel. Turn a 5mm (¼in) hem along the two raw edges of the cotton fabric. Turn a deeper hem so the pressed edge covers the seam where the net and fabric were sewn together. Pin and then stitch to create the channel for the drawstring to go through **(4)**.

Add the drawstring. Use a safety pin to help you to thread the length of t-shirt yarn through the channel as a drawstring **(5)**. Knot the ends together.

Coffee Sack Tote Bag

Some independent coffee shops will give away used coffee sacks, or sell them really cheaply. They are often printed with lovely bold designs, and the strength of the hessian makes for a perfect shopping tote.

"There are endless things you can do with hessian coffee sacks. They work really well as upholstery fabric for kitchen stools or cushions, or you could also make a version of the Denim Storage Baskets in this book."

You will need

- Old shirt
- Coffee sack
- Waistband from denim jeans
- Fabric scissors
- Sewing machine

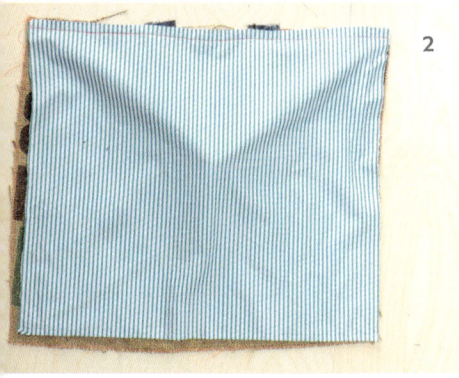

From the sack and the shirt cut four rectangles. Cut two 45 x 50cm (17¾ x 20in) pieces from each fabric. If you think your sacking is susceptible to fraying, sew a zig zag stitch around all the edges.

Make the handles. Cut the waistband carefully from the jeans. Try to cut it as close to the sewn edge of the band as possible. Cut the waistband in half. Remove buttons and belt hoops that might get in the way of stitching.

Position the first handle. Place one piece of sack fabric right side up. Along the top edge, find the centre and mark it with a pin. Fold one handle in half and place each end equidistant from the pin. Have the curve of the handle laying on the sack and the raw ends protruding by 1.5cm (⅝in). Pin in place **(1)**.

Position the lining. Place one piece of lining fabric right side down on top. Pin then machine sew along the top. Reinforce the handle areas with a second row of stitching **(2)**. Open out then press. Repeat with the other half of the bag, then place both halves together, lining to lining, outer to outer. Pin all the way round.

Sew all around. Starting at the base of the lining, machine sew all around the bag with a 1cm (½in) seam allowance. Stop 10cm (4in) before you reach the starting point to create a turning hole **(3)**.

Turn out and finish. Feed the bag through the turning hole then manipulate the layers so the lining sits inside the coffee bag. The handles will pop out. Press to finish **(4)**.

Table Tidy

When it comes to mealtimes, sweep the clutter off the table into these handy end pockets. Just don't put too much in one end or the whole thing will slide off!

"It's a good idea to work out the ideal dimensions for your table tidy using an old piece of fabric or large pieces of paper before you start. Record those measurements and adjust this project accordingly."

You will need

- Fabric scraps, at least 12cm (4¾in) square
- Scissors or ruler and rotary cutter
- Backing fabric, 50cm (20in)
- Pair of men's jeans, straight legged and as large as possible
- Sewing machine and denim-coloured thread

Work out where you want your table tidy to sit.
Measure the depth of the table, add 40cm (15¾in) to
this measurement and this will be the length of the
quilted section of the runner. We find 40cm (15¾in)
is a nice width for the tidy but adjust as you see fit.

Gather all your fabric scraps together. Ideally each
fabric piece will have straight edges, so trim away
any curved sides. Pair up different pieces along one
straight edge, then pin and machine sew with a 5mm
(¼in) seam allowance **(1)**. Press all the seams open
and flat.

Build the patchwork into 'blocks'. Sort out your
paired pieces of fabric and pair them up with other
pieces, always lining up along one straight edge. If
your joined pieces don't have straight edges, use
scissors or a ruler and rotary cutter to trim them to a
straight edge **(2)**.

To create a rainbow effect. Make blocks of similar
coloured fabric in 30cm (12in) wide strips. Cut each
block in half **(3)** so you can mirror the pattern from
the centre of the runner outwards.

Bring the blocks together. When you have enough
blocks to make the length of your runner, pin and
sew them together **(4)**. Keep an eye on the joins,
making sure the runner stays neat and rectangular
and doesn't bend off in odd directions. When all the
blocks are sewn together, trim the edges to make it
rectangular again.

Make a pocket. Cut along one side seam of each leg of the jeans. Open out and measure a 40 x 55cm (15¾ x 22in) rectangle from each leg. Ideally use the hem of the jeans as the front edge of each pocket. If you can't make this size from the legs then cut and add fabric from the rest of the jeans to make up the size. Take one of the pocket pieces, and with both the patchwork fabric and the jean fabric right side up pin together along one short edge **(5)**. Sew with a 1cm (½in) seam allowance.

Press the seams. Open out the pocket from the quilted fabric and then press **(6)**.

Complete the pocket. Fold the pocket up so the jean hem covers the patchwork fabric by about 10cm (4in). Pin both sides of the pocket. Sew up each side with a 1cm (½in) seam allowance **(7)**. Repeat with the second pocket.

To edge the quilt. Make two strips of jean fabric, each one 8cm (3¼in) wide and the length of your runner plus 5cm (2in). If you don't have enough fabric to make the strips in one piece, patchwork several smaller rectangles together **(8)**.

Turn the short edges over to make a small hem. Pin one strip right sides facing along one long edge of the runner **(9)**. Repeat with the other side. Sew with a 1cm (½in) seam allowance. Trim the excess fabric to 5mm (¼in) then press.

Backing the table tidy. Before cutting check that the lining measurents match the size of your table runner. You want to make sure that the lining is long enough to cover the edges of the denim pockets. Cut a piece of fabric 4cm (1½in) narrower and 30cm (12in) shorter than your runner. Turn a 3cm (1¼in) hem along both short edges. With the runner right side down, place the backing fabric on the runner right side up. Place it so it is central both widthways and lengthways. Pin together **(10)**.

Make the hems. On the denim border of the quilted fabric, press and turn a 1cm (½in) hem along both long edges; the denim will probably touch the edge of the lining fabric **(11)**.

Turn the hems again. This will cover the lining fabric and also the raw pocket edges **(12)**. Pin then sew along both long edges. Use a thread that is the same colour as the denim so it's not noticeable from the front. Press the whole runner well. If the pockets gape in the middle you can always divide them in two by sewing a row of stitches down the middle of each.

"Leave the pockets off this table tidy to turn it into a simple table runner. You could make different ones in a variety of fabrics for special occasions like Christmas and Easter."

Popcorn Bag

These little bags are brilliant for making popcorn in the microwave – there's no need to add oil, no washing up, and they're a great way to use old cotton fabric.

Cut and sew the material. Cut a piece of fabric 40 x 50cm (15¾ x 20in) **(1)**, fold in half with right sides facing and sew around all sides leaving a small gap to turn it out the right way.

Make the bag. Turn the bag the right way out and sew the edge closed **(2)**. This makes the flap that keeps the popping corn in. Fold the top 7cm (2¾in) of the bag over and then fold the bottom of the bag up to the top of the fold **(3)**. Pin and sew up either side and turn the bag inside out.

Shape the bag. To create a nice wide bottom for the bag, pinch and flatten the corners out to make a triangle shape, pin and sew across each one **(4)**. Now turn the right way out.

Make yourself some popcorn. To use simply fill the bag with 50g (1¾oz) of popcorn kernels. Ping in the microwave for 1½-2 minutes.

You will need

- Cotton fabric
- Fabric scissors
- Sewing machine and thread

"If you want to make more popcorn, simply make yourself a bigger bag!"

Cutlery Caddy

A quick win for reducing waste is to take your own cutlery with you, but you'll need something to carry it in. This little caddy helps keep single use cutlery out of the bin *and* reuses a plastic milk bottle too.

Marking out the case. Copy and cut out the template (*see Templates*) and place it on the side opposite the handle of the milk bottle. Often this side has measurements on it and can be a nice added design feature. The template should include a bit of the bottom of the bottle, and go around the sides. Draw around with a marker pen **(1)**.

Cut out the caddy. Use scissors to cut out the caddy, they make a much neater job than a craft knife as the plastic is quite flexible **(2)**.

Measure and make holes. Using the pen, mark holes approximately 1cm (½in) apart up each side of the cut edges and then pierce with the bradawl **(3)**. Once you have made holes in each side, hold it together and fold the bottom up inside the case, use the holes at the bottom as a guide to making a couple of extra holes in the bottom flap.

Sew together. Using a piece of yarn around 1m (1yd) long, starting at the bottom, stitch the bottom to the sides, then continue to stitch the sides together and fasten off at the top **(4)**.

You will need

- Plastic milk bottle
- Scissors
- Marker pen
- Ruler
- Bradawl
- Thick thread or yarn and suitable size needle

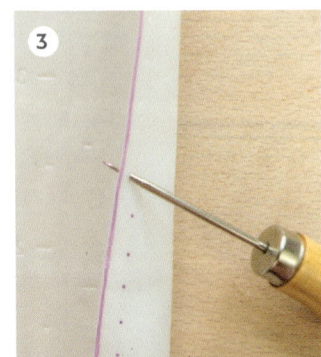

Family Pocket Planner

The little pockets on this chalkboard provide somewhere to keep those odd letters and appointment cards. You could use them to leave love notes for other members of the family or gentle reminders when it's their turn to do something. Make sure every family member has a pocket – even the pets.

"If you have collected lots of pockets you could make a giant monthly version of this planner with a pocket for each day. Add numbers to each pocket and then hang from a large cork board or piece of wood."

You will need

- Old picture frame, with a piece of thin wood cut to fit the frame
- Blackboard paint
- Washi tape
- Small cup hooks, one per family member
- One jean back pocket per family member, with a 2cm (¾in) seam allowance all round
- One jean belt hook per family member
- Pinking shears
- Fusible webbing
- Iron
- Fabric scraps
- Embroidery threads
- Bradawl

Prepare the seam allowance. On the back of each pocket iron 1.5cm (⅝in) wide strips of iron-on fusible webbing to each edge **(1)**.

Trim to neaten. Trim the denim down using pinking shears, and snip across each corner at an angle for a neat finish **(2)**.

Complete the pocket edges. Fold each seam allowance over and press with a hot iron to activate the glue of the fusible webbing **(3)**.

Decorate the pocket with each family member's name. Embroider initials with a running stitch (*see Techniques: Embroidery*) or make letter motifs using scrap fabric, attaching them with more fusible webbing. Ask each person to decorate their own. Fold a belt hook in half and hand sew it at one corner inside each pocket **(4)**.

Make the chalk board. Paint the wood with the chalkboard paint. When dry insert it into the picture frame and secure in place either with the clips from the original frame or with small nails. Use the washi tape to divide up the chalk board into sections for each family member, or the days of the week – whichever suits your family best.

Add the cup hooks. Make equidistant marks along the bottom of the picture frame, one for each pocket. Use your bradawl to make starter holes at each mark. Screw in the cup hooks and hang one pocket per hook.

Milk Bottle Storage Pots

Plastic has definitely become the bad guy of the kitchen, but it's waterproof, easy to clean, durable and flexible. Rather than dumping those plastic bottles in the recycling bin they make perfect storage containers that can go in the fridge, freezer or become a handy lunch box.

Marking out the case. Starting from the bottom of the handle, use a ruler to mark a line the same height all around the milk bottle. Drawer a curved line from each corner up to meet the line **(1)**.

Cut out the container. Use scissors to cut out the container; they make a much neater job than a craft knife as the plastic is quite flexible **(2)**.

Make rubber bands. Cut the rubber glove into 1.5cm (⅝in) strips , the fingers will make small rubber bands and the hand and wrist will make larger bands **(3)**.

Put it all together. Fold in the flaps of the pot and then use one of the larger bands to secure it **(4)**.

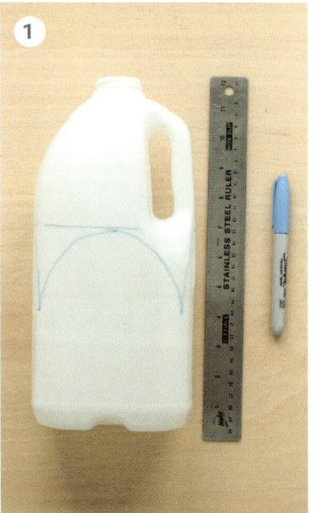

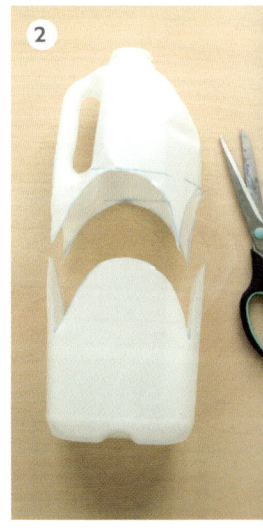

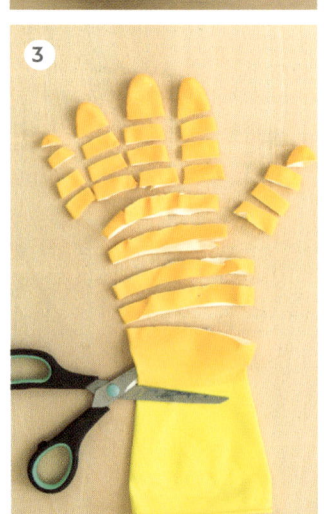

Net Curtain Bottle Washer

This is another idea that's super quick to do and works amazingly! To keep it hygienic make sure you rinse the washer out properly after use and separate out the folds of the net when you leave it to dry.

"Before making this book we never imagined how useful net curtains could be! We think they have potential for pot scourers and sieves too!"

You will need

- Rectangle of net curtain, about 15 x 60cm (6 x 23½in)
- Sewing machine
- Wooden handle, about 30cm (12in) long – a piece of bamboo garden cane, driftwood or an old wooden spoon handle. Sand one end of the stick to remove any rough edges.
- Sandpaper
- Glue gun

Take the rectangle of net curtain. Fold the two long edges to the middle overlapping them slightly. Pin **(1)**. Set your sewing machine to its longest stitch and turn off any automatic overstitching. Machine sew down the centre catching all layers of fabric.

Carefully pull the sewing thread to start gathering up the net. Keep pulling until it's all gathered **(2)**.

Fold the net in half along the stitched line. Using the glue gun fix the centre of one end of the net to the top of the wooden handle about 1cm (½in) in from the edge of the net. **(3)**.

Continue to attach the net. Carefully wind the net down and around the handle adding glue as you go to secure it in place. Keep the net quite bunched up and only cover the top 6–7cm (2⅜–2¾in) of the handle **(4)**.

TECHNIQUES

CROCHET

If you are new to crochet, hold the yarn however feels comfortable to you – if you are right-handed, hold the hook in your right hand and the yarn in your left. The abbreviations you need, and how to work the stitches, are given below.

1. Slip Knot

This is the starting point for any crochet. The simplest way to make a slip knot is to lay the yarn on a flat surface, cross the yarn over to make a loop **(A)**, pick the loop up and drop it over the tail end of the yarn to make a pretzel shape and then pull the tail yarn up through the loop **(B)**. Pull to tighten the knot and then slip the loop on to the crochet hook and gently tighten it.

2. Chain (ch)

With a loop on the hook, work a yarn over (*see below*) **(C)**, and pull through the loop **(D)**.

3. Slip Stitch (ss)

Insert the hook into the work and make a yarn over. Pull through both the work and the loop on the hook.

4. UK Double Crochet (dc)

Note that this stitch is known as single crochet in the US. Insert the hook into the stitch, yarn over and draw a loop through so that you have 2 loops on the hook **(E)**, yarn over and pull through both loops **(F)** to create the finished stitch **(G)**. Continue working as many dc as required **(H)**.

Yarn Over

To work a yarn over bring the yarn around the back of the hook and loop it over the top so that it catches in the hook.

Repeat (rpt)

This simply means repeat the stitches given between the asterisks (e.g. *2dc, dc 3*) in the pattern.

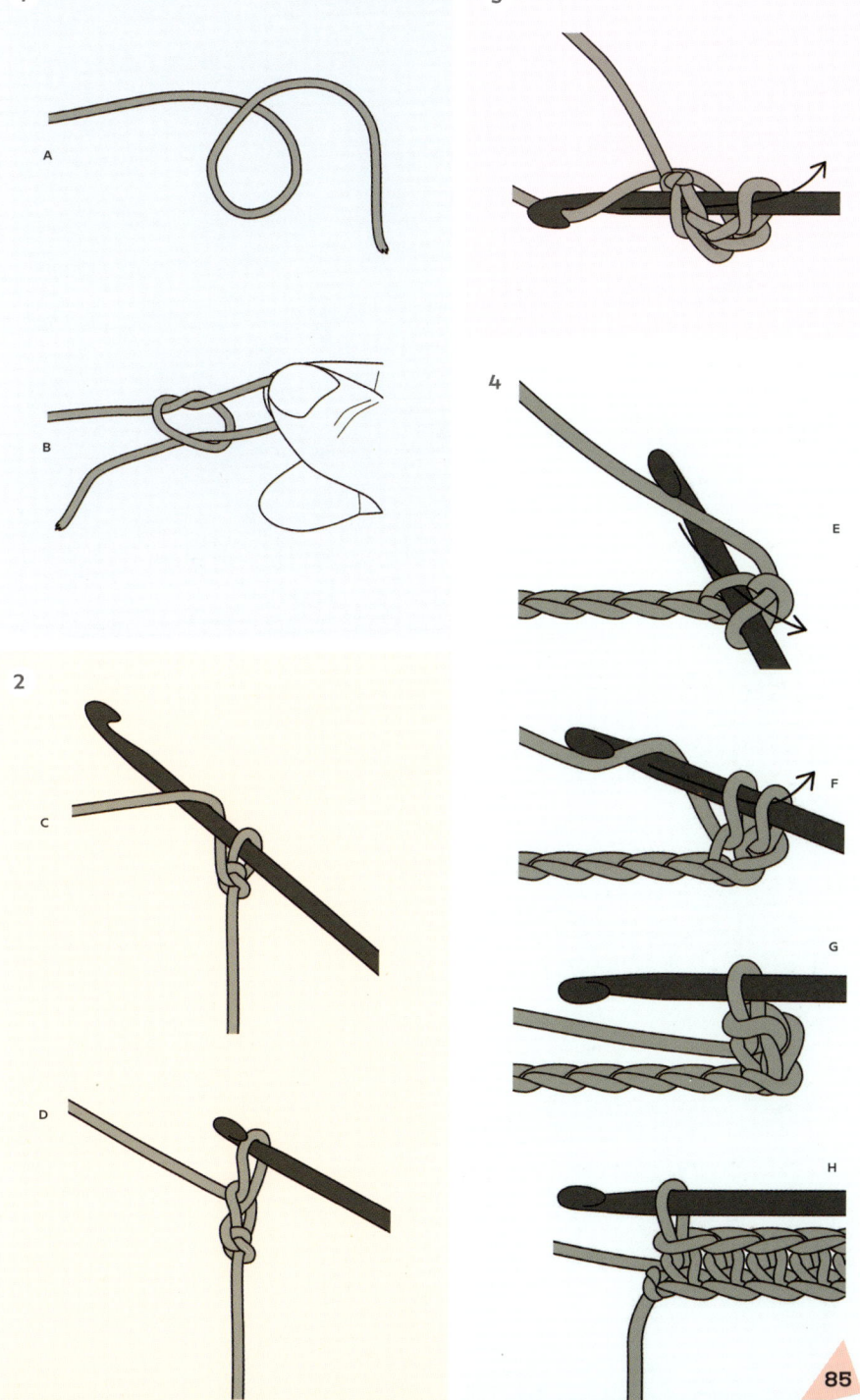

SEWING

Hand sewing has been used for thousands of years to make everything from the neanderthal loincloth to a full Elizabethan ruff and gown with hand stitched pearl edging. Sewing machines only really became common in our homes in the 1920s and, while they are a brilliant, labour-saving device, they can be intimidating and expensive; don't underestimate the power of a little needle and some thread! Here are some general sewing techniques that can send you on your way to nicely finished and durable makes (and they can be done by hand or on a sewing machine).

Hemming

When there's an instruction to 'hem the edge' it usually means a double hem. This is where you fold the raw edge over, press (or sew) it in place, fold it over and sew it down. This catches all the threads from the raw edges and tucks them neatly inside the hem.

Topstitch

This is a technique that is used when the stitching is designed to be seen and can be functional or decorative. It's usually just a neat row of stitching run around the top of an edge, like a neckline or the top of a bag, to keep things in place and add detail.

Running Stitch

This can be done on a machine or by hand and it is the simplest of stitches: needle goes in, needle comes out a little further along, repeat and that's it.

Tacking (Basting)

This is the same as a running stitch but usually long and loose. It's used to hold things roughly in place, and is then snipped and removed afterwards. Sometimes it's helpful to do this in a contrasting colour to the thread you are going to sew with. This makes it easier to identify and remove later.

Cutting

Knowing how to cut fabric is really helpful as it will stop things getting distorted as you snip. The way to do it is to move your hands and not the scissors – lay the fabric out flat and then, as you cut, keep the bottom blade of the scissors touching the flat surface and move your hand to cut and turn the scissors.

As with everything, a little practice makes perfect.

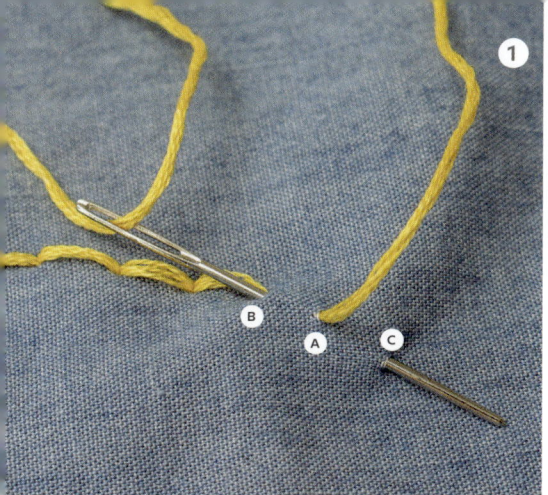

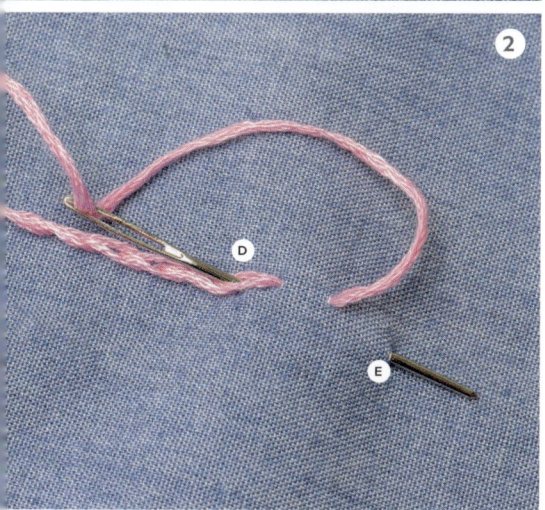

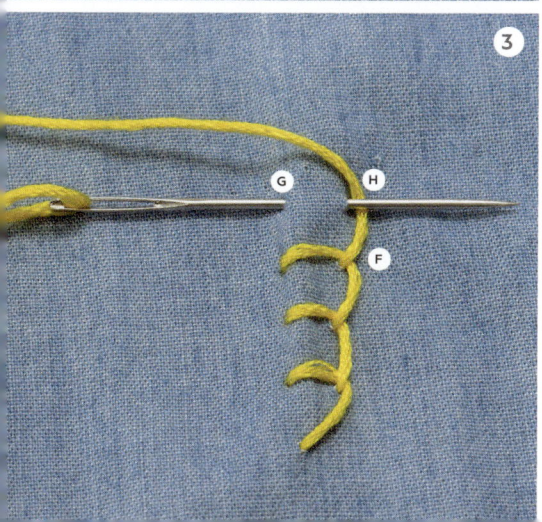

EMBROIDERY

1. Back Stitch

Bring up your needle from underneath your fabric at **(A)**, stitch backwards to **(B)** and then bring your needle out at **(C)**. Insert the needle back at **(A)**, and continue along the line.

2. Split Stitch

Working with a stranded embroidery floss, bring up your needle from underneath your fabric and make a back stitch, insert the needle at **(D)** through the middle of the previous stitch, splitting the thread. Bring the needle back up at **(E)** and continue along the line.

3. Blanket Stitch

Bring up your needle from the back of the fabric at **(F)**. Insert the needle at **(G)** and bring it out at **(H)**. Make sure you loop the thread around your needle before you complete the stitch.

T-SHIRT YARN

You can now buy big reels of stretchy cotton yarn made from selvedge fabric leftover from the t-shirt making process. However, making your own is a really easy process and super satisfying too. Ideally look out for t-shirts with no side seams (the fabric is a tube) and a high cotton content – 100% cotton or a cotton polyester mix work well. Try to avoid shirts with a screen printed pattern as this can make your yarn a bit stiff.

Begin by cutting away the sleeves and the neck from the body of the t-shirt **(1)**. Try and cut so the body is as big a rectangle of fabric as it can be. Unpick the hem of the shirt and the sleeves.

Place the t-shirt fabric on a flat surface. Lay it so the cut edge is to your right and the unpicked hem is to your left. Fold the bottom of the fabric up to about 3.5cm (1¼in) from the top edge. Starting at the base cut 2cm (¾in) wide strips vertically as shown **(2)**. Stop each cut about 3cm (1⅛in) from the top of the shirt.

Manipulate the shirt so the uncut portion is uppermost (so it looks a bit like a spine and ribs!). Starting at the right hand side cut diagonally from the edge of the tube across to the first cut as shown **(3)**, this releases the first bit of yarn. Continue cutting diagonally across each strip from the previous cut to the next until you've cut them all.

You should now have one long continuous piece of yarn. With your hands, stretch the strips taut to make them curl up **(4)**, this makes the yarn even longer and look better.

The template on this page is shown at 25%. You can download full-size versions of the templates in this book from **www.davidandcharles.com.**

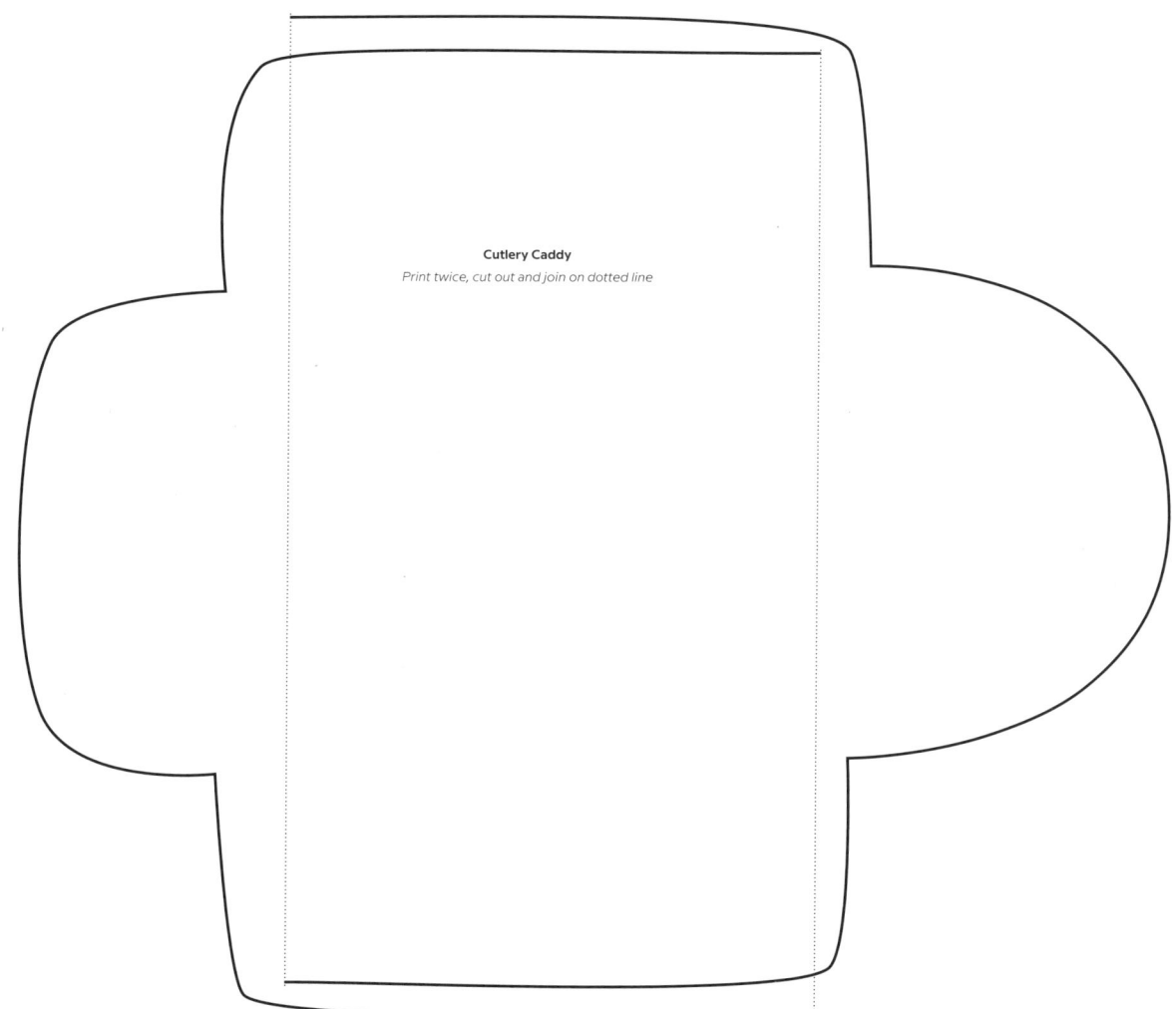

Cutlery Caddy
Print twice, cut out and join on dotted line

TEMPLATES

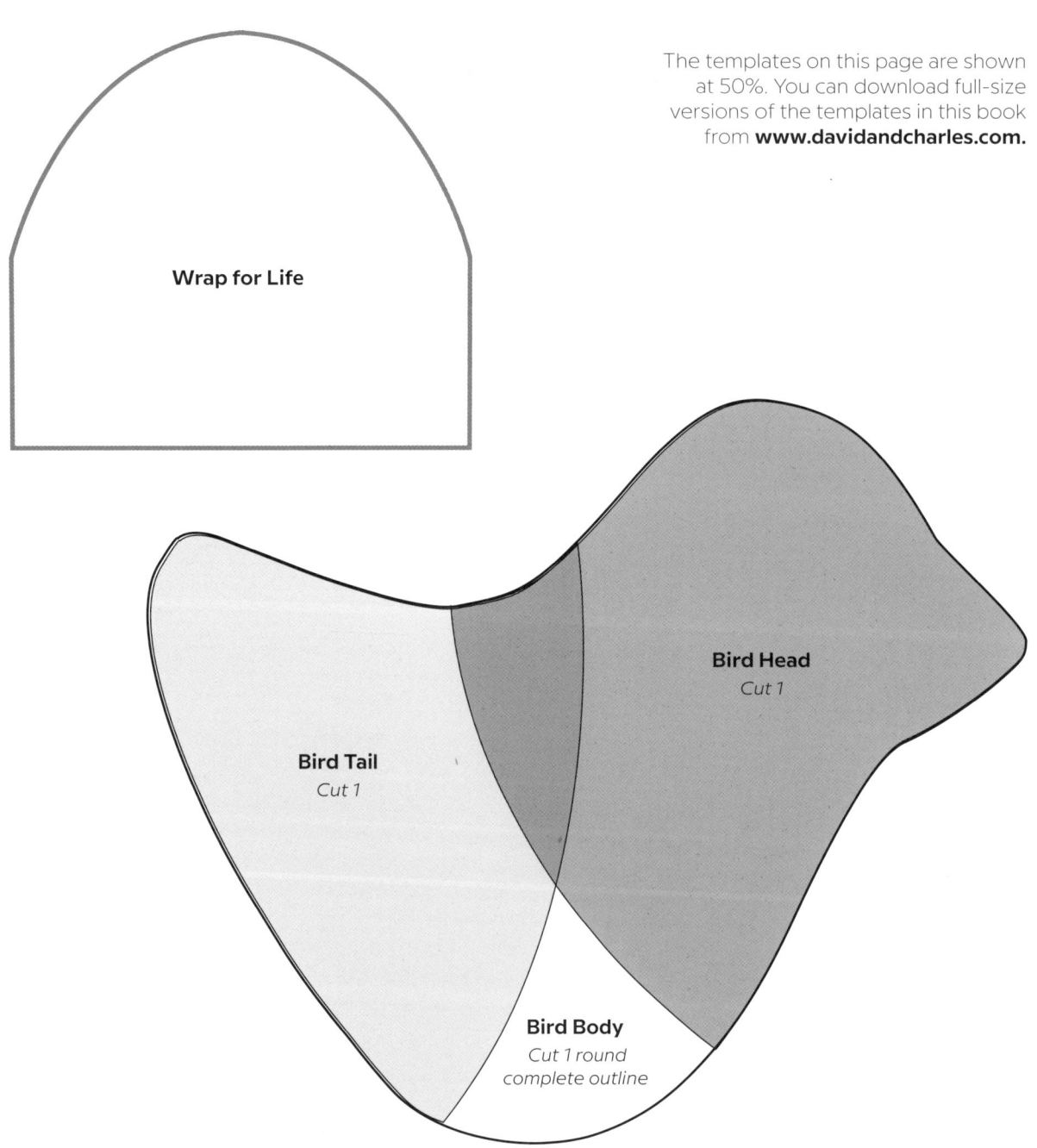

Wrap for Life

The templates on this page are shown at 50%. You can download full-size versions of the templates in this book from **www.davidandcharles.com.**

Bird Head
Cut 1

Bird Tail
Cut 1

Bird Body
*Cut 1 round
complete outline*

Suppliers

Looking for healthy glues or perhaps a bit of extra fabric? Here's what we do:

Friends and neighbours. Asking for donations is a great way to gather interesting fabric for projects. It will save your friends and neighbours a trip to the charity shop, especially people with young families who grow out of things at a crazy speed!

Charity Shops. High Street charity shops are a great place to shop. Look for extra large garments, sheets and towels for maximum fabric gain. You'll often find some vintage treasures which can make excellent material for aprons, cloths and packaging.

Thenewcrafthouse.com. All the beautiful fabrics on this website are designer deadstock – destined for landfill or stored away for years and forgotten about. It's a constantly changing line up of fabrics.

Textilegarden.com. All the buttons you could ever want including a lovely selection of eco and recycled ones.

Greenstat.co.uk. The Green Stationery Company have a selection of earth-friendly glues and sticky tapes (perfect for those that might want to eventually compost or recycle their creations) as well as all the usual things you'd find at a stationer's.

Wrap.org.uk. This source can be a little dry but is a great place to find factual info and advice about everything from upcycling fabric to what to do with your food waste.

Inspiration

We find a lot of inspiration on Instagram and love connecting with people on a visual level. Here are some great accounts to follow all doing their thing for the environment:

@sewyeah The place where Christine documents her crafty life.

@steelandstitch Emma specialises in awesome clothing and crochet hacks.

@katiejonesknits Crazy and colourful knitting and crochet patterns. Katie is a strong supporter of workers' rights in the fashion industry and is all about sustainability.

@enbrogue A brilliant account full of tips on how to live a more sustainable life, from clothes shopping to vegetable patches.

@makeitbettermag Conscientious crafting for the modern maker. Full of inspiring makes and how-tos all with a 'reduce, reuse, recycle' vibe.

@makesmthng Greenpeace's crafty cousin – using maker-power to fight overconsumption.

@zerowasthome Bea Johnson's zero waste journey, making everything from her own eyeliner to leftovers soup.

@zerowastenerd shares super cute listicles and illustrations to help you cut down on waste and live a little greener.

@the.endery specialists in using up leftovers, they also showcase some beautiful mending

About the Authors

Christine

Christine Leech is an author, designer, maker, stylist, and workshop host. She won her first craft-related award at just 5 years old (best hemmed handkerchief in the village Flower Show). This led to a life filled with cardboard, fabric, scissors and glue.

This is her eleventh book and her second in the Zero Waste Craft series. The first, *Zero Waste Gift Wrap,* is filled with beautiful projects for sustainable wrapping.

She lives by the adage *'A Creative Mess is Better Than Idle Tidiness'* which gives her the excuse to never tidy up! She documents her crafty life on her Instagram @sewyeah, where she shares daily inspiration, step-by-step projects and videos.

Emma

Emma's first foray into upcycling was at nine years old when she turned her curtains into a Ming the Merciless dressing gown. At 39 she came full circle and got an MA in Sustainable Design (but didn't use her curtains this time).

Over the last 10 years she has written numerous books on crochet, craft and upcycling and is a regular contributor to UK craft mags and websites. She loves teaching and has run workshops all over the country, from The Clothes Show to her children's primary school.

Emma is passionate about sharing ways to transform everyday materials with the power of craft, and lots of these can be found on her instagram @steelandstitch.

Our thanks to...

We would both like to thank Sarah Callard for believing in Zero Waste Living, the role craft can play in making a difference and commissioning this book. Anna, Jason, Jess, Pru and Jane for making it look beautiful, sound right and feel lovely.

Emma would like to dedicate this book to her Dad who actively encouraged her to take down the curtains when she was nine and turn them into a dressing gown, and will always be a part of everything she makes.

Christine would like to thank everyone who keeps her going on her crafty journey. Her friends and family and all the usual suspects.

We would both like to thank everyone who buys this book and in doing so moves one step further towards a more sustainable lifestyle and a happier planet.

Index

A DAVID AND CHARLES BOOK
© David and Charles, Ltd 2021

David and Charles is an imprint of David and Charles, Ltd
Suite A, Tourism House, Pynes Hill, Exeter, EX2 5WS

ISBN-13: 9781446308714 paperback

ISBN-13: 9781446380789 EPUB

We have considered the environmental
impact of this book by using soy-based inks,
printing on FSC paper and using unbleached,
uncoated duplex board for the front cover.

Printed in China by Asia Pacific for:
David and Charles, Ltd
Suite A, Tourism House, Pynes Hill,
Exeter, EX2 5WS

10 9 8 7 6 5 4 3 2 1

Senior Commissioning Editor: Sarah Callard

Managing Editor: Jessica Cropper

Project Editor: Jane Trollope

Head of Design: Anna Wade

Art Direction and Styling:
Prudence Rogers

Book Layout and Design: Anna Wade

Photography: Jason Jenkins, Christine Leech
and Emma Friedlander-Collins

Pre-press Designer: Ali Stark

Production Manager: Beverley Richardson

David and Charles publishes high-quality
books on a wide range of subjects.
For more information visit
www.davidandcharles.com.

Layout of the digital edition of this book
may vary depending on reader hardware
and display settings.